# Life's Universal Clockwork:

## How to Reprogram Your Life and Increase Happiness Even Though Life Isn't Fair or Easy

*Brittnay A. Baltazar*

Copyright © 2017 – Brittnay A. Baltazar
All rights reserved.

No part of this book may be reproduced, distributed, or by any means, including photocopying, recording, or other electronic or mechanical methods without written permission of the publisher.

**ISBN-13:**
**978-0692884270 (Baltazar Partners, LLC.)**

**ISBN-10:**
**0692884270**

# *Dedication*

I wrote this book to pay-it-forward to not only my family, but to your family as well.

I thank my wonderful husband, Michael Baltazar, for empowering me to continue to strive for peace, joy and love! Thank you for loving me so greatly and for being an awesome business partner! Love you forever and ever, Babe!

Thank you to all my wonderful kiddos for giving me the power and strength to write this book and to strive to help others!

Thank you to all those who have helped make this book possible! You rock!

Lastly, I would like to give all the glory to God for this book and for my life! Thank you for loving me and helping me grow in all areas of my life!

# Table of Contents

**Introduction** .................................................................................... 7

**Part One:**
**Understanding the Clockwork of Your Life** ........................................ 8

**Chapter 1 – What's Making Your Life So Hard?** .............................. 9
    Focusing on the Past ............................................................... 10
    Pretending the Past Never Happened .................................... 13
    Blaming Others for Your Shortcomings ................................. 14
    Trying to Change Others ......................................................... 14
    Understanding Yourself Is the First Step Toward a Better Life ...... 15

**Chapter 2 – Life Is Unpredictable – So How Is It Like "Clockwork"?** . 18
    Most of Your Problems Are Recurring and Predictable ............. 19
    Self-Sabotage in Relationships ............................................... 20
    Self-Sabotage and Addiction .................................................. 21
    Self-Sabotage and Self-Control .............................................. 22

**Chapter 3 – You Don't Need a New Life – Just a New Time Clock** ..... 25
    A New Time Clock for Your Romantic Relationships .............. 26
    A New Time Clock for Coping with Bad News ....................... 27
    A New Time Clock for Personal Development ....................... 29

**Part Two:**
**Learning to Reprogram Your Life and Creating a New Time Clock** ... 33

**Chapter 4 –**
**Refocusing – Getting Away from the Past and into the Present** ...... 34
    Confront Your Regrets ........................................................... 35
    Forgive Yourself ..................................................................... 35
    Get Busy with Positive Activities ............................................ 36
    Consciously Bring Yourself Back to the Present ..................... 38

Practice Positive Self-Reflection ................................................... 38
Keep Your Goals in Mind .............................................................. 39

## Chapter 5 – Accepting the Things and People You Can't Change ...... 42
Re-Evaluate Your Expectations ...................................................... 43
Don't Try to Suppress or Ignore Your Feelings ............................... 45
Don't Argue with Irrational People ................................................ 46
Learn to Identify What You Can't Change ..................................... 46
Don't Focus on What You Can't Change ........................................ 47

## Chapter 6 – Learning to Control Your Thoughts and Words ............. 50
Be Conscious of Your Thoughts ...................................................... 51
Quell Your Inner Critic .................................................................... 52
Take a Breath Before You Speak ..................................................... 52
If You Don't Have Anything Nice to Say ......................................... 53
Make an Effort to Say Positive Things to Others ........................... 54

## Chapter 7 – Dealing with Addictions,
## Guilty Pleasures, and Other Instant Gratifications ......................... 57
How Do You Want to Be Remembered? ........................................ 58
Identify What Drives You to Your Guilty Pleasure ......................... 59
Replace Bad Habits with Good Ones ............................................. 60
Will This Make You Feel Good Now or Later? ............................... 60
Let Go of Guilt ................................................................................ 61
Stay on the Right Path After Rehab ............................................... 61

## Chapter 8 – Discovering the Universal Clockwork System
## and Enjoying the Benefits of Reprogramming Your Life .................. 64
What is the Universal Clockwork System? ..................................... 65
Gain Access to a Lifestyle Where Everything Comes Together ...... 66
The World Loses Its Sting ............................................................... 66
Experience Less Pain and Fewer Unpleasant Surprises ................. 67
Notice New and Wonderful Things You Never Saw Before ........... 68
Events and Situations Change,
    but the Clockwork Remains the Same ....................................... 69

## Chapter 9 – Seven Steps to Improve

**the Clockwork Events of Your Life ................................................... 71**
    1 - Reprogram Your Mind: Garbage In, Garbage Out ..................... 72
    2 - Reprogram Your Heart ................................................................ 74
    3 - Reprogram Your Voice ................................................................ 75
    4 - Develop Techniques to Protect Your Mind, Heart, and Voice ... 76
    5 - Reprogram Your Outlook and Expectations ............................... 77
    6 - Create a System of Self-Accountability ..................................... 78
    7 - Share Your Story with Others .................................................... 79

**Conclusion ................................................................................................ 80**
    Be Patient and Stay the Course ....................................................... 80

    Works Cited ....................................................................................... 83

## Introduction

Do you feel like your life is too hard? Do you dwell on your past mistakes and long for the days when things were simpler and life was more fun? Are others constantly disappointing you when they don't live up to your expectations? If you answered yes to one or all of these questions, you're not alone.

These questions all exhibit very human traits that most people display. Though they're incredibly common, these traits may be holding you back from experiencing a simpler, happier, and more peaceful life. If you can learn to live in the present and focus on the future instead of focusing on the past, to re-examine your expectations of others, and to accept the things and people you can't change, then you'll be on your way to an easier and more fulfilling life.

You see, whether you know it or not, your life works much like clockwork, even when it feels incredibly unpredictable. As a human, you're a creature of habit, and you show habitual, predictable reactions to problems and challenges in your life. When you can understand the clockwork of these situations and your reactions, you'll see the path to better problem solving, less stress, and happier relationships.

In this book, we're going to walk you through the concept of life as a clockwork system and your personal time clock for coping with that system. Then we'll discuss how you can reprogram your time clock to reap the benefits of the universal clockwork system instead of fighting against it and finding yourself in a never-ending cycle of self-sabotage. You'll learn how to break the cycle and reprogram your mind, heart, and voice to be a more caring and centered person – a real person with a more fulfilling life.

**<u>Are you ready to reprogram your life? Let's get started!</u>**

# Part One:

## Understanding the Clockwork of Your Life

# *Chapter 1*

# *What's Making Your Life So Hard?*

> *"Stop focusing on how stressed you are and remember how blessed you are."*
> - Author Unknown

If you're having a hard time with your job, your relationships at home, your finances, and/or your health, you may be sitting there thinking, "Why does life have to be so hard? Why isn't it ever simple?" Well, we may not have a good answer for *why* life is so hard at times, but we can help you figure out why it *seems* so hard sometimes while it seems like a breeze at other times.

Believe it or not, your life may seem harder and more complicated than it is because you are succumbing to a few very human traits. If you dwell too much on the past, blame others for your problems, and focus too much on trying to change them instead of trying to change yourself, you're going to have a hard time. That's not to say that you are a bad person for exhibiting these traits or that you are at fault for trying to help change others. However, focusing on these things will hold you back from enjoying a simpler, more peaceful life.

In this chapter, we're going to look at each of these traits very honestly. As you read through the next few sections, try to be as reflective and open as possible, so that you can see where you exhibit these traits and how they may be affecting your life negatively. Once you can honestly admit to doing these things, you will have taken the first step in reprogramming your life and creating a more tranquil and easier system for yourself.

## Focusing on the Past

Do you often find yourself thinking about the good old days? Whenever you're having a bad day or having difficulty at work, do you think of a mistake you made years ago that changed your life? Do you think, "If only I had chosen differently, I wouldn't be in this situation"? Focusing on the past can negatively affect your life in a couple of different ways.

**Nostalgia's Double-Edged Sword**
This is not at all uncommon. In fact, it's such a common human trait that almost everyone you meet exhibits it to some extent or another. Some people idolize their younger years. "College was the best time of my life!" they say, as they tell the same stories of their youthful antics over and over again.

While they may seem happy in regaling you with their former "glory," if you look a bit closer, you'll notice something interesting. As their story winds down, note that they probably seem just a little bit sad and that they might even sigh or frown for a moment before they launch into another tale of "the good old days." Why does this happen? How is being nostalgic about a good time in your life bad for you?

Consider what your friend said at the beginning of their first story about college antics. They said that those were the best years of their life, and when you look at that statement logically, you can see why it's a little bit sad. It means that they've never felt as good or had as much fun since those four years in their late teens and early twenties. Nothing in their life, including meeting and falling in love with their spouse, building a career, starting a family, or any other worthwhile endeavor will ever stand up to the way they view their college career.

There's nothing wrong with looking back fondly on good experiences, but if you believe that those years were the best of your life and that you'll never experience better times than those, you're setting yourself up to feel constantly disappointed and stressed. You're telling yourself that it's all downhill from here and that you might as well just focus on the past, when things were better.

See how nostalgia can be a double-edged sword? See how it can set you up to feel like life is hard and like you'll never have an easier or better time again? Be careful when you wax nostalgic about a certain time in your life, because chances are good that it wasn't as perfect as you remember and that you don't have it as bad now as you think in comparison. Remember the grass on the other side always looks greener, till you get to the other side and you realize all it is, is artificial turf...

**"If Only I Had..."**
Now, you may not be stuck in the past, wishing for better days, but you may be focusing too much on mistakes and choices you made years, months, or even just weeks ago. Maybe you didn't take a risk to join a new startup company that then took off and made millions. Maybe you embarrassed yourself in front of your boss when you didn't have the right file formatting for a presentation. Maybe you waited to talk to someone you had a crush on, and by the time you got up the nerve, they were already happily in a relationship with someone else.

As humans, we often reflect on our decisions and their cause-and-effect nature. Reflecting on these decisions to learn from them and determine our next move is a great trait that will get you through a lot of hard times in your life. However, focusing and dwelling on your past mistakes will only make you miserable.

For example, let's say that you get some bad news at work. Instead of dealing with it in a healthy manner, you decide that you need a drink. You go out to a bar with a couple of friends because misery loves company, and you proceed to get drunk for several hours. When you wake up in the morning, you have a terrible headache. The details of the night before are blurry, and you realize that you can't remember driving home. You walk outside and see your car in your driveway, and it hits you that you not only acted disrespectfully to others while you were drunk, but you also put yourself and others in danger by driving while intoxicated.

You immediately feel regret, and you swear to yourself, "I'm never doing that again." Unfortunately, if you focus on the mistakes you made getting drunk and acting out, you may actually be setting yourself up to do all of those things over again the next time you get bad news or have a difficult situation to deal with.

The better way to deal with this is to admit that you made a mistake and move on with a plan to prevent it from happening in the future. Instead of saying, "Next time, I won't get drunk," you can say, "Next time, instead of getting drunk, I'll go home, cook myself a good meal, and go for a run to clear my head." This thought process replaces the problematic behavior with a positive solution. It allows you to forgive yourself for your mistake and move forward, and it gives you a better coping mechanism for the next time this kind of behavior is triggered.

So, you can see how focusing on even the very recent past can get you in trouble. Whether you're feeling guilty about getting drunk when you should've been doing something productive, or you're still lamenting a decision you made years ago, you're exhibiting a very human and understandable trait that can make your life feel much more difficult and complicated. If you can stay in the present and forgive yourself and others for past mistakes, you'll be on your way to a simpler and more fulfilling life.

## Pretending the Past Never Happened

At the other end of the spectrum, some people simply refuse to acknowledge their mistakes from the past. They try to convince themselves that they've done nothing wrong and made no mistakes. This really isn't any better than dwelling on the past because, when you pretend that the past doesn't exist, you are robbing yourself of the opportunity to learn from your mistakes and become a bigger, better, and stronger person.

To illustrate this, let's take the same example from above. However, instead of dwelling on the mistakes you made by getting drunk and acting out, you simply say, "I didn't do anything wrong," and you refuse to acknowledge anything that might be off about how you reacted to the bad news at work, how you treated your friends or others, or even that you drove home drunk. You think to yourself, "Well, I'm fine. Next time I probably won't have so much to drink, but, really, I got home safe, so nothing really bad happened, right?" You know this is wrong, but you refuse to believe it.

Instead, you convince yourself that you don't have a problem. By pretending that everything is okay and that your past does not have any effect on you, you deny yourself the ability to grow, and you will continue to make your life harder.

## Blaming Others for Your Shortcomings

No one wants to be the bad guy, and no one ever wants to admit when they've made a mistake. If we all had our way, we'd never make poor decisions, feel jealous, overreact, or have other poor reactions to difficult situations. Because of this trait, as humans we tend to divert blame to others. Instead of admitting that you might have done something wrong, it's much easier to blame someone else.

Continuing with the above example, many people will blame their boss for giving them the bad news that sent them into self-destructive behavior. Or they'll blame their buddy for enabling them and buying them one too many drinks. In either situation, if you can swallow your pride and admit your own shortcomings or mistakes, you'll be in a position to learn from those mistakes and to work on your weaknesses. If you just blame others for your situation, you'll have no opportunity to grow or give yourself a better life.

## Trying to Change Others

Finally, instead of owning up to our own responsibilities and working to change ourselves, we will often attempt to change others. We may believe that we're trying to change them to make their lives better and to help them become better people, but this is actually not the case in most instances. Instead, when we look closely at our efforts, we can see that we're trying to change them for our own selfish means so that they'll fit more into our *perception* of the way things are and how life should be.

Let's say that you have a friend who is following a different career path than you. You tell yourself that you're worried about them and that they're making poor decisions, so you constantly interject yourself into their life to give them unwanted advice and to try to steer them in the direction you've chosen for your life.

If you've ever done something like this, think about why you really did it. Was it because you were truly worried about your friend? Or were you jealous that they were taking a risk you weren't willing to take? Were you sad that their schedule wouldn't allow more time for the two of you to hang out? Did you feel like your friend was making poor decisions because those decisions would lead to trouble or difficulties, or did you feel that way simply because they weren't the decisions *you* would have made?

Whether your intentions were completely pure or more selfish (as is most often the case), at some point you need to realize that changing others is impossible. True change comes from within, and taking it upon yourself to change someone else will only bring you heartache. It'll make your life much harder, as you'll be too focused on someone else and the problems you perceive for them than dealing with your own problems and responsibilities.

## Understanding Yourself Is the First Step Toward a Better Life

Do any or all of these traits sound familiar to you? If so, you're definitely not alone. Like we said, they're all very human and very common, so there's no reason to feel bad or guilty for having them. Instead, you just need to learn to reprogram your mind and your life so that you can diminish these traits or even rid yourself of them completely.

In the next chapter, we'll explore how life – as unpredictable as it can be – is often like clockwork, and how you can improve your life by understanding and reprogramming your clockwork responses to different situations. Then we'll move on to discuss how creating a simpler and easier life is all about changing your personal time clock for your life.

*Take a few moments now to use this page as a time for self-reflection:*

## Chapter 2

## Life Is Unpredictable – So How Is It Like "Clockwork"?

*"History repeats itself endlessly for those who are unwilling to learn from the past."*
– Leon Brown

At this point, you've done some reflecting, and you've been honest with yourself. You understand that a lot of the things that make life seem more difficult and complicated come from a few basic human traits that you exhibit every day. However, when we say that life is like clockwork, what do you think?

If you're like a lot of people, you automatically think, "Well, sometimes it can be, but life is so unpredictable. How can you say it's really like clockwork?" Yes, life can be unpredictable. Your alarm may not go off when you could've sworn that you set it the night before. You may unexpectedly get sick. Your boss might suddenly cut your hours at work, creating a major financial problem for you.

These things happen unexpectedly, but in most cases your *reactions* to these situations are actually very predictable. In essence, you create the clockwork of your life in the way you deal with unpredictable situations in a very predictable manner. Confused? Let's explore this concept a little deeper.

## Most of Your Problems Are Recurring and Predictable

As humans, we are creatures of habit. We tend to react to similar situations the same way every time, and, when we exhibit the human traits we discussed in the last chapter, we tend to self-sabotage and create the same problems for ourselves over and over again.

Let's say that you get some bad news at work, so you go out drinking and show up late the next day. Leaving aside the problem of drunk driving (let's say, in this case, you took a cab home and retrieved your car in the morning), are you preparing yourself to deal with the situation at work by getting drunk and then showing up hungover the next morning? Of course not. In fact, by doing this, you're not only failing to deal with the situation in a healthy manner, but you're also sabotaging yourself.

When you do this over and over again, you will eventually lose your job. Then, when you get a new job and you find out that things aren't perfect there either, you exhibit the same behavior over and over again until you lose that job as well. The cycle continues, and while the individual problems may differ, the overall situation is very predictable due to your unhealthy coping mechanism of getting drunk instead of handling the situation in a healthy manner. It's easy, from here, to develop an addiction and to go further down the path of self-destructive behavior to make your life even harder than it is now.

This is not the only way that people self-sabotage, though. In fact, this kind of repeated behavior occurs in handling relationship issues, dealing with addictions, and all kinds of other areas of our lives. Let's take a look at a different example, one in which you keep finding yourself in failed romantic relationships.

## Self-Sabotage in Relationships

When you first started dating, you probably didn't have a lot of trust issues or problems opening up to the person you were with, right? However, over the years, as you've had a few bad experiences along the way, you picked up a few coping mechanisms to try to shield yourself from getting hurt again. These mechanisms, when you strip them down, though, are often just those same traits we discussed in the last chapter. They're disguised versions of focusing on the past, blaming others, or trying to change others, and they will actually do more harm than good in the long run.

For example, let's say that you were married and your spouse cheated on you. Since then, you've had a very hard time trusting others. As a result, because you don't want to be fooled again, you constantly look for signs that your significant other is cheating. You look through their phone, their browser history, and their Facebook messages. You show up unexpectedly to "surprise" them, but you're really there just to see if they've invited someone else over since they weren't expecting you.

This kind of behavior shows your significant other that you don't trust them and that you can't let go of the past to build a future together. Soon they break up with you because you're so obsessed with finding out if they're cheating that you constantly break their trust by snooping and showing up unannounced.

Furthermore, people who have been betrayed in the past, who continue to hold onto that betrayal, tend to gravitate toward people who are untrustworthy. They continue to date the same type of person over and over again, so they're more likely to be betrayed again. In this case, they self-sabotage by continuing to go down the same path over and over again, choosing the same type of partner and then spending more effort on trying not to be surprised by betrayal than on actually trying to build a healthy relationship.

From this example, you can see how you make your life predictable through your actions and reactions. In this case, you are not doomed to continue to date cheaters and people who will betray you if you stop the cycle. You have the power to reprogram your life and change the way you react to give yourself a better chance at healthy relationships in the future.

## Self-Sabotage and Addiction

Now, let's talk about addiction. People don't wake up one morning and decide to start an addiction. They don't say, "I think I'll start binge drinking until I can't function without alcohol in my system," and they don't say, "I think I'll try shooting up heroin today. That sounds like a good idea."

In fact, most addicts *want* to stop using drugs, drinking alcohol, obsessively watching pornography, or doing whatever it is that's hurting themselves and their loved ones. However, their addictions are not only physical – they're mental and emotional as well. In the example we discussed throughout the last chapter and this one, we were looking at someone who was either developing or had already developed an alcohol dependency.

In this situation, whether or not this person had a physical dependency on alcohol, what was the first thing they did when they got bad news? They went to the bar, and they didn't just have a drink or two – they got drunk. And then they engaged in regrettable and dangerous behavior. The next day, they swore they'd never do it again, but what happens the next time they get bad news? If they don't replace alcohol with a better coping mechanism, then they'll go directly back to drinking.

If you have ever struggled with an addiction, then you likely already know how easily you can self-sabotage, but you may not recognize it when you do it. When you've been clean for a few days or weeks and you have a relapse, it's easy to think something like, "I might as well just keep getting high because I've already messed up." That thought is a clear example of self-sabotage.

As we mentioned earlier, humans are creatures of habit, and we program ourselves to react in certain ways to different situations. This programming can lead to addiction, and it can keep us addicted through self-sabotage like this. Fortunately, with help and some reprogramming, you can break the cycle, replace your bad habits and addictive behaviors with healthier coping mechanisms, and completely change your life.

## Self-Sabotage and Self-Control

This same programming can hurt you with any number of endeavors in your life. For example, let's say that you're trying to lose weight. You've always been a little bit overweight, and being overweight has become a part of how you see yourself. You believe that you're overweight because you have no self-control or discipline, so you try to put yourself on a harsh, restrictive diet. When you fail, you reconfirm for yourself that you have no self-control and that you'll never get the body you want because you'll always fail.

Do you see how much this situation is like the person who's been betrayed in romantic relationships? And how much it resembles the addict who uses a relapse as an excuse to quit trying to get clean? On the surface, these situations and examples may seem very different, but when you look at them through the lens of your predictable, repeated reactions and your programming, you can see how much alike they are.

You can see, now, how life is like clockwork in the ways your reactions to different situations create a predictable cycle. That may seem somewhat depressing at first, but it's actually very good news. Consider this: in every one of these situations, with the right reprogramming, you have the ability to break the cycle and make your life simpler and easier.

That's the point of this book, and it's why we talk about creating a new time clock for your life. When you think of it this way, you'll see your problems more clearly and you'll see how you can reprogram your life to have a time clock that's more real and in tune with the world around you - a time clock that's a better reflection of your heart and soul, rather than a reflection of a tainted view of the world and others.

**DON'T LET HISTORY REPEAT ITSELF!**
At this point, you may still feel like you would rather have a whole new life and a clean slate to start over on, but that's not true at all. In fact, that's a reflection of your old programming, focusing on the past, blaming others, and trying to change things and people that are out of your reach. In the next chapter, we'll go into more detail about why you don't need a new life and how you just need a new time clock.

***Take a few moments now to use this page as a time for self-reflection:***

# Chapter 3

## You Don't Need a New Life – Just a New Time Clock

*"You must master a new way to think before you can master a new way to be."*
- Marianne Williamson

Now, despite realizing that your life has followed a set of patterns that work a lot like clockwork, you may be sitting there thinking that there's no way to get out of the cycle and get a fresh start. You're probably wishing that you could start over with a clean slate, knowing what you know now, so that you could break the cycle before it started, right?

Guess what – when you wish for a new life because you regret the decisions and mistakes you've made, you're just dwelling on the past. You're focusing on what you've done wrong instead of looking at what you can do differently in the future.

In reality, you don't need a new life. In fact, the life you have is actually probably a lot better than you think it is, and you can make it even better with a new time clock. Simply by changing your personal time clock to react in more positive ways and change yourself instead of dwelling on your mistakes or trying to change others, you can improve your life by leaps and bounds. Let's take a moment to see what it would look like if you changed your time clock in just one area at a time, starting with your romantic relationships.

## A New Time Clock for Your Romantic Relationships

Whether you've been cheated on in the past, you've always gravitated toward codependent relationships, or you've experienced some other form of negative romantic relationship over and over again, there's a reason for this. You might think it's because your ex betrayed you or couldn't do anything without you. However, when you blame others for your failed relationships, you deny yourself the opportunity to grow and change.

We're not saying that it's your fault that someone cheated on you, and we would never say that a victim was to blame for abuse. However, once you get away from a cheater or an abuser, you have the power to stop the cycle, break the chain, and keep yourself out of the same kind of relationship again.

Let's say that one of your exes cheated on you. Like a lot of people looking for love, companionship, and affirmation, you probably didn't take enough time to heal after that heartbreak. Instead, you went out looking for someone else who could show you love the way that your ex couldn't.

Unfortunately, that betrayal left a scar on you, and now, because it happened once, you feel like you're unworthy of love and like it's going to happen over and over again. This is when you start looking over your new partner's shoulder when they're texting with someone else. It's when you start snooping on their computer and looking through the pictures on their phone. It's when you start invading their privacy because you're afraid that they'll hurt you like your last partner.

This is a very common reaction, but if you change your time clock, you can stop it. Instead of going out to find a replacement for your cheating ex, you can take some time to be by yourself, to get counseling if you need it, and to do the things you need to do to see that you're worthy of real love and that it wasn't ever your fault that your partner cheated.

Once you find this inner peace and healing, you'll be in a position to open yourself up to truly trust someone else again. Of course, it's not as simple as just taking some time off from dating, but we'll get to *how* to reprogram your time clock in the next chapter. For now, let's just look at what it looks like when you change your time clock and your reactions instead of dwelling on problems and trying to change others. In the next example, we'll look at what it looks like when you change your time clock for dealing with bad news.

## A New Time Clock for Coping with Bad News

Have you ever been fired from a job? Has your boss ever come to you and told you that the company is going through cutbacks and that they need to cut your hours? Has someone you love ever told you that they don't want to see you anymore? Have you come home one day to find out that your rent is going up or your roommate is moving out unexpectedly?

Bad news comes in all shapes, forms, and sizes, but it's not the news that determines how your life will go after you receive it – it's your reaction. If you have a healthy coping mechanism for receiving bad news at work, at home, or in any other part of your life, you'll be able to take these hurdles in stride.

Let's say that your boss comes to you one day and tells you that you need to really improve your performance or you'll be fired. If you're like a lot of people, you probably thought your performance wasn't that bad and that you didn't have anything to worry about. Now you know that you're going to lose your job if you don't improve. How do you react?

If you're like a lot of people, you probably immediately feel anger toward your boss. They just can't see how much work you've been putting in, and it's not your fault… But is that true? Have you been putting in all of the effort you should, or have you been letting your work slide? Should you really be feeling angry at your boss?

If you don't take the time to ask yourself these questions, you'll likely continue to carry that anger with you throughout the day. Then, when you go home, you're likely to act out in a self-destructive and self-sabotaging way. Instead of considering what you can do better and taking steps to improve your performance, you go out drinking with one of your friends, and then you show up for work late and hungover the next day. Will you be surprised when you lose your job?

What if, instead of placing the blame on your boss and acting out in a self-sabotaging way, you decided to take this warning as motivation? When your boss comes to you and tells you that your performance needs to improve, instead of getting angry and/or clamming up, you ask if the two of you can sit down to discuss your performance and the specific places it's lacking. Then you can find out together if there's a gap in your training, if there was a misunderstanding of responsibilities, or if there's some other way that the two of you can work together to do a better job and make everyone happier.

After this conversation, you'll feel more relieved than angry, and you'll be more likely to go home and go for a run or hit the gym to blow off steam. You'll have a plan forming in your head for how to boost your performance, and you'll be motivated to get to bed early, get up and get to work on time, and to put your plan in action.

All this comes from a simple shift in your personal programming. Even if you've always dealt with bad news at work or at home by drowning your woes or acting out in a way that you regret later, you don't need a whole new life, just a new time clock.

## A New Time Clock for Personal Development

In the last chapter, we briefly discussed self-control and discipline. These words come up a lot when people want to get in better shape – as we discussed – or when they want to learn a new skill or habit. They're also often used in relation to addictions. This kind of language can actually be very damaging if you're stuck with your old time clock. Why? Because addicts and people who are overweight are often told that they don't have any self-control or discipline.

They're told that if they develop these traits, they'll be able to kick the habit or stick to their diet and get the results they want. However, getting those results — whether we're talking about getting clean or losing 50 pounds — is much more difficult when you haven't programmed your life so that you know how to react in times of stress, anxiety, anger, or sadness.

For many people, relapsing or cheating on a diet isn't just about wanting to get high or wanting to taste something delicious. It's an emotional response to a triggering situation. If you're told that you're a fat slob and that you'll always be one, your first reaction is likely going to be to make yourself feel better. And, as counter-intuitive as it might seem, that means you'll likely want to eat some comfort food. Whether it's cake or mashed potatoes and gravy, you'll crave these foods because they make you feel better (at least for a moment).

When you give in to those cravings, you'll of course almost immediately feel worse about yourself, and you'll feel as though you're doomed to continue this cycle forever, never getting where you want to be. At some point, you'll probably think, "Why even try?" and decide to give up on your diet entirely.

Instead, what if you reprogrammed your personal time clock to have a different reaction when you hear hurtful words like those? What if you were able to brush those words off and continue doing healthy things to make yourself feel better? If, instead of feeling hurt and diving into a pint of ice cream, you thought about why that person was saying something terrible, you might find yourself in a different position.

Suddenly, seeing that you're doing just fine and that this person is just trying to hurt you, you don't feel as hurt anymore. In fact, you feel like you must be doing something right, and so you continue with your efforts to better yourself.

You can't change others, and you can't always please others. When you begin to understand that, thanks to your efforts to reprogram your time clock, you'll have better coping mechanisms and better habits to fall back on. You'll reflect on why you do the things you do, and you'll look to your long-term motivations to determine whether or not you should react in a certain way.

So how can you reprogram your life? How can you reset your time clock to stop the cycle of self-sabotage and give yourself the simpler, more peaceful life you've been dreaming of? In the first part of this book, we've focused on why your life is like clockwork even when it's unpredictable, and why reprogramming your life and creating a new time clock will help you. In the next part, we'll get into *how* to do that reprogramming.

**Take a few moments now to use this page as a time for self-reflection:**

# Part Two:

# Learning to Reprogram Your Life
# and Creating a New Time Clock

## Chapter 4

## Refocusing – Getting Away from the Past and into the Present

*"Don't let the concept of change scare you as much as the prospect of remaining unhappy."*
– Author Unknown

The first step in reprogramming your life is to get out of the past and into the present. That's easier said than done, of course, as you probably find yourself ruminating on past events almost every single day. Whether you look in the mirror and immediately think about how thin and svelte you once looked or you keep going over and over a conversation with your boss from a week ago, you're not helping yourself.

Ruminating on the past, whether you're reminiscing about how good things used to be and how great you used to look or you're analyzing and overthinking every mistake you've made – you aren't doing yourself any favors. In fact, when you do this, you're just wishing that you could change the past (or live in it), and we know that's not possible. Basically, you're wasting energy and making yourself miserable, and this can lead to more poor decision making and a continued cycle of hardships in your life. So, what can you do?

## Confront Your Regrets

First, for just a moment, think about the things you regret most in your life. Confront them head-on and reflect on *why* you have these regrets. Then, instead of saying, "If only I had…," ask yourself, "What do I want?" In general, you don't actually regret your specific actions, inactions, and decisions – you regret the effects of those decisions. You regret that you're not in a better place mentally, emotionally, and physically, and you believe that changing something in your past would put you in that desired emotional and mental space.

Guess what – even if you change every mistake you've ever made, you'll still have regrets. Everyone does, and that's okay. Instead of focusing on the things that you regret, in this instance, think about where you want to be now, in a month, in six months, in a year, and in five years. Instead of thinking about how your past actions ruined your chances for happiness (they didn't), think about how you're going to change your actions now to create a healthy mental, emotional, and physical space for yourself.

## Forgive Yourself

Once you've confronted your regrets, take some time to truly forgive yourself for your mistakes and poor decisions. You did not ruin your chances for happiness, and in fact right now you're doing the work necessary to achieve that happiness and meet your goals, no matter what mistakes you've made in the past.

Forgiving yourself can be much harder than forgiving others, but try to think of the times you've forgiven friends and loved ones. Treat yourself as you've treated others. Look in the mirror and say, "I forgive you." It might sound silly at first, but you might be surprised at how effective it can be.

But why is forgiveness so important? You've been sabotaging yourself for years by basically holding a grudge against yourself for your past mistakes and decisions. You can't move forward to start loving yourself and reprogramming your life until you let that grudge go.

By not forgiving yourself, you are basically telling yourself that you are not worthy of forgiveness and that you might as well continue to make the same mistakes and act out in the same self-sabotaging ways because there's no hope for you. Well there *is* hope for you. So, cut yourself some slack and learn to let go of your old mistakes and forgive yourself.

## Get Busy with Positive Activities

What do you think about when you go to the gym or when you go for a long run? What goes through your mind when you're working on a cool crafting project, practicing yoga, meditating, or helping feed the homeless? When you engage in positive activities like these, your brain is too busy in the moment to focus, dwell, or ruminate on the past.

If you're running, taking a Zumba class, lifting weights, or kickboxing, your mind is too busy keeping your body going to think about your past mistakes. Then, when you finish with your session, you feel so good about yourself for doing it and you have so many endorphins flowing through your body, that your past mistakes are the farthest thing from your mind.

That's why so many people advocate getting some exercise when you're feeling down or stressed. However, as great as it can be, exercise isn't the only positive activity that can help you overcome your fixation on your past.

Positive hobbies like crafting can be a lot like meditation. During the time that you're creating something cool and useful, you're focused on the task at hand, not on the problems in your life and where they came from. Knitting, sculpting clay, drawing, making furniture, or coming up with a fun pipe cleaner crafting project with your kids will have you focused on creating something new, not dwelling on past problems.

Then, when you're done, you'll have something to show for your time. You'll have the satisfaction of creating something useful and beautiful for yourself or others, which can go a long way toward making you feel better about yourself. When you create something with your own two hands, you'll feel more capable of creating solutions to the problems in your life, and you'll feel motivated to tackle them instead of wishing they'd just go away.

Finally, we mentioned feeding the homeless because charitable acts have a wonderful way of refocusing us as humans. When you work in a soup kitchen or volunteer at a women's shelter, your mind will not only be taken up by positive tasks and activities, but you'll also get a better perspective on your life by seeing what others are going through. Giving your time to others is one of the best ways to give yourself a break from the past.

The more you practice these positive activities, the better you'll feel about yourself and the more you'll focus on them and other positive things in your life. Before you know it, you'll find yourself thinking less and less about the past and more and more about the future.

## Consciously Bring Yourself Back to the Present

Of course, sometimes, when you least expect it, a thought or memory will pop into your head. Suddenly, you'll be thrown back into thinking about the past and replaying bad memories over and over. This often happens when you're idle or when you're trying to relax and unwind before bed, and if you let it, it'll keep you up all night and prevent you from maintaining a quality connection with your present and the positive things you're doing for yourself.

When this happens, be conscious of it. Instead of replaying that conversation with your boss again in your head, switch gears and think about what you need to do to get ready for a good day at work the next day. Instead of wishing that you still looked as slim as you did in your younger years, think of the positive, healthy things you're doing now to become stronger and healthier than ever.

## Practice Positive Self-Reflection

It's easy to say, "I hate my wrinkles," or "I wish I were thinner," and no one ever seems to have a problem saying, "I wish I'd said something different." These are examples of the negative self-talk that plays throughout most people's heads all day long every single day. These little slights and insults will chip away at your self-confidence if you don't do anything about them, and before you know it, you'll be back to wishing you could change the past.

Fortunately, though, you can fight all that negative self-talk by practicing positive self-reflection. In the mornings, when you look in the mirror, make a point of noticing something you love about yourself. Then say out loud something like, "I'm beautiful, and I deserve great things." When you're getting ready for bed at night, think of the positive things you did for yourself and others that day and the things you'll be doing the next day to continue making your world a better place. Before long, this will be habit, and your negative self-talk will all but disappear.

## Keep Your Goals in Mind

Remember, whether you're taking on new art lessons or a new workout regimen, you're not trying to get back to the past. You're not trying to reclaim your youth or fix the mistakes you made long ago. Instead, you're building a beautiful present with a bright future.

If you fill your time with positive activities, consciously push yourself to stay focused on the present, and practice positive self-reflection, the past will stop lurking in the back of your mind as much. Plus, when you do these things, you'll be taking the steps you need to create a better life for yourself, and you'll have reprogrammed a large part of your life before you even know it.

Of course, staying in the present isn't the only thing that most people need to reprogram about their time clocks. Most of us have a tendency to try to change others, and we have a hard time accepting the things and people we can't change. By focusing on others' shortcomings and trying to change them instead of changing ourselves, we do ourselves and them a disservice.

In the next chapter, we'll discuss how to reprogram your thinking toward others so that you can accept the things and people that you can't change and focus on changing yourself for the better instead.

## Let's take some time and make a list of some of your life goals:
**(Post these goals and affirmations up where you can read them every day to yourself)**

1 month:

_____
_____
_____

6 months:

_____
_____
_____

1 year:

_____
_____
_____

5 years:

_____
_____
_____

Make a list of 5 daily affirmations:

_____
_____
_____
_____
_____
_____
_____
_____
_____
_____
_____
_____
_____

# Chapter 5

## Accepting the Things and People You Can't Change

*"If you are not in a state of either acceptance, enjoyment, or enthusiasm in everything you are doing, then you are creating suffering for yourself and others."*
*- Eckhart Tolle*

Accepting that you can't change others and that there are some things and situations in your life that you can't change can be one of the most difficult things to do. However, if you can learn to let go and stop trying to change things and people that are out of your control, you'll find that life gets a lot simpler and easier. While you still face the same struggles, challenges, and hurdles, you'll have a better perspective on how to solve your problems when you focus on yourself and the things you can change.

What happens when you accept the things and people you can't change? You'll find it easier to maintain a positive attitude. You'll worry less, and you'll feel less stressed, even when dealing with a particularly challenging situation. You'll feel more energetic, as you won't be wasting your energy trying to take on the impossible task of changing others. Plus, you'll find that you can embrace change more readily and go with the flow when you need to adapt.

So how do you do all that? Here are a few of the best tactics we've found for learning to accept what and whom you can't change.

## Re-Evaluate Your Expectations

First of all, whether we're talking about a coworker, spouse, friend, or family member, consider for a moment what you expect from this person. Let's say, for example, that you ask your spouse to take the trash out to the curb each week the night before trash pick-up day. Every week, no matter how many times you ask, they seem to forget. This makes you angry, and you're tempted to act in a passive aggressive manner toward them until they learn their lesson and get better about it. But is that a positive way to address the situation? Of course, it's not, even if your spouse never remembers to take the trash to the curb.

Now, instead of pestering them over and over to take the trash to the curb and getting mad when they forget, let's take a step back and look at the situation, your spouse, and your expectations. In your mind, you do a lot around the house and you keep up your end of the bargain with chores and responsibilities, so they shouldn't have a problem doing this one thing. However, marriage is not a cut and dry contract between two people. Just because you mow the lawn or do the dishes doesn't automatically mean that your spouse is in charge of the trash.

If your spouse is a bit scatterbrained and has trouble remembering schedules, taking the trash out may be a difficult thing for them to remember until trash day has already passed. At the end of the day, you're both tired after a long day of work, but you can create a more positive space for your relationship by doing a few simple chores together, like cooking, cleaning the dishes, taking the trash out, and/or starting a load of laundry. And you can talk openly about how to divide up the chores in a way that's fair to both of you.

For whatever reason, the person you love and have decided to spend your life with can't seem to remember to take out the trash. Yes, it's frustrating, but is it really a reason to get angry and hold a grudge? If you keep blaming your spouse for your frustration and trying to change them instead of looking for a better solution, it could wreak havoc on your relationship.

This is a pretty simple example, but you can use it in all kinds of situations. You can't control your coworkers, your boss, or anyone else in your life. So, when you have a problem with them, before you get angry or frustrated, take a moment to re-evaluate your expectations instead of spending a lot of energy trying to get them to act the way you think they should. When you take this step back, you'll start to see other solutions to the problem instead of continuing to waste your time and energy trying to change someone else.

## Don't Try to Suppress or Ignore Your Feelings

That being said, if someone is acting in a way that frustrates or angers you, it does you no good to ignore your feelings. If you feel like you're being taken advantage of, you do not have to continue to take on more work and/or let someone take credit for the things you've done. If you feel that someone is taking advantage of you or if something they do habitually makes your job harder, first re-evaluate your expectations to ensure that you're not the one who's taking advantage in this situation.
Then, once you have a better perspective on the situation and the other person's role in it, if you can't find a good way to solve the problem, you have a choice. You can confront that person about their behavior and try to work with them to find a solution that works for both of you, or you can cut them out of your life.

If we're talking about a coworker, you're likely going to have to figure out how to work together effectively, but what if we're talking about a friend? What if you're making changes in your life, and you want your friend to change, as well?

Let's say that you're working to handle stress, bad news, and other situations without alcohol or drugs, and your friend has always been an enabler and a drinking buddy. When you tell them that you want to clean up and live a healthier life, they may show some verbal support, but what do you think they're going to do the next time you see them and either of you has gotten some bad news? They're likely going to invite you out for a drink to blow off some steam.

Then, if you say no, they're just going to say, "Aw, come on. Just one drink!" Instead of getting them to change, if you ignore your own feelings in order to spare theirs, and you keep them in your life, they're going to interfere with your own change. This is a case in which it's often better to say goodbye (at least for now) so that you can work on changing yourself instead of trying to change someone else.

## Don't Argue with Irrational People

With this in mind, there are times when you may not need to walk away from a person entirely but you most definitely need to walk away from an argument or debate. People get passionate and irrational when it comes to things they care deeply about. If we're talking about religion, parenting, or politics, you're not likely to make any headway in telling someone that your way is better. In fact, there's a good chance that you're being no more rational or logical than they are, but you both feel as though you're right, and you're going to get nowhere with the argument.

Instead of butting heads, it's better to gracefully bow out. This will save you a lot of time, stress, and anxiety, and it'll save a lot of relationships in your life, as well. Accept that others have different points of view and don't try to force them to be like you, and you'll have a lot more time to focus on the improvements and changes that you *can* affect in your life.

## Learn to Identify What You Can't Change

You already know that you can't change people's personalities and habits. However, you might not have a really good grasp on the things and situations that you can and can't change. You might think that you hate your boss but you can't change your job situation. Well, that's not entirely true.

Yes, you might actually hate your boss, and no, you can't change him or her to be a different person whom you'll like better. However, you can change your job situation, and that doesn't necessarily mean leaving your current job.

However, when you identify that you can't change your boss' personality, you can look at the situation as a whole and pinpoint exactly what makes you miserable in this situation. Is it that your boss is just a terrible person (something you can't change)? Or is it that your boss is under pressure from the company's executives, and you're constantly late turning in deliverables?

Your boss may not be a bad person, and they may not even have a bad personality. They may just be under a lot of pressure, and you may be making their job harder. In this situation, either getting on the ball with your deliverables or improving your communication with your boss about why you need more time on deadlines will change your situation dramatically for the better.

## Don't Focus on What You Can't Change

Now, having said that, whether we're talking about a person or a situation, if you can't change it (or them), you shouldn't be focused on it. Practice looking at the things and people you can't change as fixed objects in a landscape. When you set off on a hike, you don't try to walk through trees, hills, or boulders – you find paths around them that lead you to beautiful vistas and a sense of great accomplishment.

If you aren't happy with a situation you're in, sit down and start writing down lists of the things you can and can't change. You can't change that you have a very different personality than your boss or one of your coworkers and that you wouldn't be great friends outside of work.

You can change how you address these people at work and the attitude you approach them with. You can't change that someone is scatterbrained and has trouble remembering dates and schedules, but you can account for that when you work with them (or live with them).

You'll find that practicing positive activities, as you did to learn to stop dwelling on the past, will help you with this as well. Now, you'll find that a lot of what we covered in this chapter has to do with how you interact with others. Trying to change someone can lead to hostility, while recognizing that you can't change them and working with them toward a solution can create harmony.

If you want to create more harmony than dissonance with others in your life, you'll need to learn to control your thoughts and words, which we'll review in the next chapter.

***Take a few moments now to use this page as a time for self-reflection:***

_____
_____
_____
_____
_____
_____
_____
_____
_____
_____
_____
_____
_____
_____
_____
_____
_____
_____
_____
_____
_____

# Chapter 6

## Learning to Control Your Thoughts and Words

*"One of the happiest moments in life is when you find courage to let go of what you cannot change."*
*– Author Unknown*

By now you know that you can't change others and that you need to accept the things you can't change in order to live a happier and simpler life. In the last chapter, we discussed some examples of this and how to deal with situations in which you might be tempted to try to change someone else instead of looking to yourself and the things you can change for a solution.

If you want to do this regularly, and if you want to make it a part of your time clock, you'll need to learn to control your thoughts and words. Here are a few of the best tips for reprogramming the way you think and speak.

## Be Conscious of Your Thoughts

First of all, as you go through your day, all kinds of thoughts will pop into your head. By default, many of us compare ourselves to others almost unconsciously. If you see someone who's in better shape than you are, you might feel a little bit down. Instead of just acknowledging that this person is either genetically blessed or spends a lot of time working out and eating right, you'll look them up and down, notice their bad haircut, and chuckle to yourself about it.

This kind of reaction is unpleasant, but it's not uncommon. Every day, we rank ourselves against others, and when we don't measure up, we look for ways to tear others down. Doing this actually doesn't do anything good for you because it forces you to denigrate others to make yourself feel better. However, this is how society programs us, and it's how many of us cope with our own shortcomings – by focusing on the flaws of others. And we do it without even thinking about it.

So here's your challenge to begin reprogramming the way you think. Be conscious of the thoughts running through your head. Evaluate whether they're positive or negative. If you find yourself laughing at someone's poor fashion sense, bad haircut, or weight, stop yourself. Consciously put that thought out of your head and find something kind that you could say about that person. As you go through your day, paying attention to your thoughts, make an effort to think positively and to focus on the good things about the people you meet and think about throughout your day.

The more you practice this, the more your thoughts will gravitate toward the positive traits and aspects of others and the less you'll focus on their shortcomings. This will help you see them in a new light, and it'll help you relate to them in more positive ways as well.

## Quell Your Inner Critic

Now, those negative thoughts don't just apply to others. We touched on negative self-talk earlier, but we should revisit it here also. After speaking with your boss, talking to someone you have a crush on, giving a presentation, or doing anything else that causes you to feel anxious or stressed, you're likely going to go over it again and again in your head. Replaying a conversation once in your mind to get the most important parts and learn from the experience isn't a bad thing, but going over it again and again just so that you can criticize every word you spoke and action you took isn't healthy.

When you find yourself wincing at something you just said, comparing yourself negatively to a better-dressed coworker, or otherwise criticizing yourself, make a conscious effort to stop, just like you would do when thinking negative thoughts about someone else. Replace those negative thoughts and criticisms with something positive. Then refocus your thoughts on the things you need to do today, and move on. Keep practicing this, and it'll become more and more routine.

## Take a Breath Before You Speak

Of course, thoughts aren't all we need to control. You also need to focus on what comes out of your mouth and how it affects others. If someone comes to you with a proposal for a new way to do part of your job, what do you say? If you're in the habit of speaking before you think, as so many of us are, you're likely to blurt out the first thing that comes into your head, which may not be a good choice.

Why not? When someone approaches you with a proposal for change, you're going to almost automatically react negatively because, as humans, we're wired to resist change. Even if the idea is great, your first reaction might be to say, "That's idiotic!" At work, this could result in poor working relations and/or disciplinary action. In your personal relationships, it can lead to hurt feelings, breakups, and strained friendships.

On the other hand, if you pause and take a breath before you speak, you'll have a moment to consider what you're about to say and how to say it.

## If You Don't Have Anything Nice to Say…

Now, even if you take that moment and consider what you think on the subject, it may still be better not to share your exact thoughts. When you were a kid, your mom probably told you at one time or another, "If you don't have anything nice to say, don't say anything at all." Well, that old saying still stands for adults, but we often forget it and plow ahead with inconsiderate words that hurt others instead of building them up.

What do you think it does for you when you tell someone that their idea is idiotic? Whether they're a friend, colleague, employee, or anyone else, they're going to feel hurt when you say something like this, and that feeling is going to taint the way they see you and how they interact with you in the future.

On the other hand, if you can say something constructive and considerate, they'll likely respect your opinion and want your input on improving their idea or concept. Even if they don't appreciate what you have to say now, they will eventually appreciate how you handled the situation and the tact and kindness you used to convey your thoughts. And if they don't, others will.

Furthermore, if someone keeps goading you to get a reaction out of you, there's nothing wrong with keeping quiet and walking away.

This often feels like you're giving in and letting them "win," but it takes a very big person to know when to shut their mouth and avoid harsh words that they'll regret later. If you abide by this old rule, you'll do great things for yourself in both your business and personal life.

## Make an Effort to Say Positive Things to Others

Knowing when to shut your mouth and when not to say exactly what's on your mind will stand you in good stead professionally and personally, but you can do even better than that. Consider those people who always have something nice to say when you meet them. Even if they just have a bright smile to give and a nice, sincere, "Hey, how've you been?" your day is suddenly better after talking with them.

It's funny, also, that these people always seem to be in a better mood than others in the same situation. That's because being positive and spreading good cheer can actually put you in a better mood and help you relax so that you can deal with difficult situations more effectively with less stress.

If you consciously make a point to say something positive and kind to the people you meet, interact with, and work with on a daily basis, you'll notice a significant difference in your mood, your job satisfaction, and your relationships. Doing this will not only help you practice keeping your thoughts more positive, but it will also make others more comfortable around you, which will make it easier to relate to them and work with them.

Now that we've covered how to reprogram your thoughts and words, let's move on to talk about some of the most difficult behaviors to change. Addictions, guilty pleasures, and other instant gratifications can make you feel good for a moment while wrecking your self-esteem and self-image in the long run. Not only that, but they can lead to some of the worst decisions of your life. In the next chapter, we'll discuss how to build more self-control and handle these problems better by reprogramming your time clock.

***Take a few moments now to use this page as a time for self-reflection:***

# Chapter 7

## Dealing with Addictions, Guilty Pleasures, and Other Instant Gratifications

*"When the devil keeps asking you
to look at your past,
there must be something good in the future
he doesn't want you to see."*
- Author Unknown

Addiction is one of the most difficult things in the world to control and live with. Whether you're addicted to alcohol, drugs, tobacco products, or anything else, you always have this sneaking feeling in your mind and heart that you're hurting yourself and others whenever you partake. At the same time, it's so easy to say, "I'll just have one drink," or "I'll just have one smoke." You rationalize using and indulging because you get instant gratification from your habit.

However, that gratification won't last. In fact, it may be gone just minutes after you take the last drag on that cigarette or as soon as you sober up from that "one" drink (which inevitably turned into many more).

When you succumb to the temptation to indulge in addictions and guilty pleasures like this, you're sacrificing your future happiness to feel better right now. You know that you're hurting yourself and the people you love when you do this, and you know in your heart that what you're doing is wrong. It's just so difficult to stop, though, when you have a physical, mental, and/or emotional dependency. So, what can you do? Try practicing these tools and exercises to look at the big picture and see a better life for yourself with delayed gratification.

## How Do You Want to Be Remembered?

First, when you're tempted to do something that you know is destructive, take a moment to think about how you would want to be remembered if this was your last day on earth. There was a story in the newspaper a few years back about a man who died of a heart attack at a Circle K. The details of the story included that this man – who was 48 and married – was at the Circle K with his girlfriend (who didn't know that he had a wife) at the time of his death.

No matter what else this man did with his life, the newspapers printed the details of his last few moments (which weren't exactly flattering), and his case isn't unique. Consider all of the drug overdoses you hear about on the news. Those stories are about real human beings, but all the world will ever remember about them is that they died of an overdose. By choosing drugs, they leave behind a legacy that they'll never have the chance to recover from.

While the faces in these stories change, the story itself remains the same — like clockwork. Fortunately, for many people, just taking a moment to think of their family and their legacy can get them moving back in the right direction. It's only a start, though, and without practicing the next steps to remain sober and to make better decisions, it may not hold up against the physical and emotional cravings that come with a serious addiction.

## Identify What Drives You to Your Guilty Pleasure

In most cases, people don't just start overeating, binge drinking, popping pills, or smoking cigarettes because they think it's a good idea. There's usually a trigger that sets them off and puts them on the path of instant gratification. Do you smoke when you're feeling stressed and you need a break? Do you eat when you feel sad or angry? Do you drink when you feel overwhelmed?

Identify the emotional and situational triggers that drive you to partake, and you'll be one step closer to finding a better way to deal with these issues. For example, if you figure out your trigger, instead of saying, "I want a cigarette," you can say, "I'm feeling stressed, and I need to step away for a moment." Then you can take a walk (without a smoke) or take a few minutes to sit quietly and meditate until you feel more relaxed and ready to deal with the world again.

## Replace Bad Habits with Good Ones

After you've identified what causes your cravings, you can start replacing bad habits with good ones. When you feel triggered to drink, instead of heading to the bar, you can put on your running shoes and hit the pavement for a couple of miles. Every time you want a cigarette, take a lap around the office instead of stepping out for a smoke. If you're tempted to hit the vending machine or dive into a cake when you're feeling sad, grab a piece of fruit and call a friend to tell them you love them.

Trying to kick bad habits to the curb without replacing them will leave empty holes throughout your day, and it's easy to fill those back in with the same bad habits (or new ones). If, instead, you fill those holes with good habits, you'll have no room to backslide.

## Will This Make You Feel Good Now or Later?

When deciding whether or not to do something, like have a drink, eat a high-calorie snack, or go outside for a smoke, you can keep yourself on the right track by asking yourself, "Will this make me feel good now or later?" If you eat a candy bar now, you'll feel good about that sugary taste now, but as soon as it's gone you'll still feel hungry, and you won't feel so great about yourself.

On the other hand, if you grab an apple instead, you'll not only enjoy its juicy flavor, but you'll be more energized and you'll feel better about yourself when you're finished, too.

If you take a smoke break, you might indulge your craving and feel a buzz while you're smoking, but then you'll have to live with yourself the rest of the day, with the aftertaste of smoke on your breath and the smell on your clothes. You know it'll make you feel good now, but how will it make you feel later?

## Let Go of Guilt

That said, as with letting go of the past, you have to forgive yourself when you do slip up. If you give in to peer pressure to smoke or go out for drinks when you know you'd be better off going for a run or hitting the gym, don't beat yourself up. Forgive yourself and take some time to think about how you'll do better next time. Again, don't just say, "I won't do that again." Instead, figure out what you'll do instead.

For example, instead of meeting your friends for drinks at a bar, you could recommend meeting at a coffee shop or going for a hike. And, if your friends won't let up on you for quitting smoking or drinking, remember that you can't change them. The solution may be to cut them out of your life, at least until you are strong enough to say no.

## Stay on the Right Path After Rehab

Before we move on to the next chapter, in which we'll talk about the benefits of discovering the universal clockwork system and reprogramming your life, we should point out that if you have a physical addiction to drugs or alcohol, rehab and counseling may be necessary. There's no shame in getting professional help if you need it. In fact, this can be one of the first steps in reprogramming your time clock.

Professional counselors and rehabilitation clinics will give you a lot of the tools you need to get clean, but maintaining a healthy and happy life afterward is up to you. With the tools we've laid out in this chapter, you can continue on the right path, whether or not you need professional help with your addiction.

We're not purporting to be a substitute for rehabilitation or counseling. However, once you've gone through your initial treatment, come back to this chapter and see how these habits can help you continue on the path to reprogramming your time clock so that you can avoid relapsing, stand up to peer pressure, and continue to improve your life.

*Take a few moments now to use this page as a time for self-reflection:*

_____
_____
_____
_____
_____
_____
_____
_____
_____
_____
_____
_____
_____
_____
_____
_____
_____
_____
_____
_____

# Chapter 8

# *Discovering the Universal Clockwork System and Enjoying the Benefits of Reprogramming Your Life*

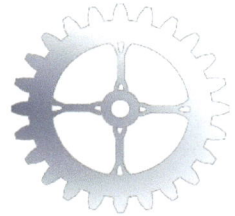

*"In order to love who you are,
you cannot hate the experiences
that shape you."*
-Andrea Dykstra

Now that we've discussed how life is like clockwork, even when it's unpredictable, and we've gotten into detail about how you can reprogram your personal time clock to reprogram your life, let's go into a bit more detail on the universal clockwork system and the benefits you can enjoy from reprogramming your life.

Sometimes, simply knowing that there is a universal clockwork system and reading about the ways you can enjoy a better life can be motivation enough to get started.

## What Is the Universal Clockwork System?

First of all, though, you're probably wondering about how there could be a universal clockwork system. You understand that your own life works like clockwork, based on the ways you react predictably to different situations and how those reactions perpetuate cycles. You understand that a lot of your currently programmed reactions are self-sabotaging, and you know that reprogramming your time clock can help you.

So is it really that surprising to learn that the whole universe works the same way? Consider it this way. Your work life is like clockwork, and so is your home life. They work together (or against each other, depending on your time clock) to make your whole life work like clockwork.

The universe is the same way. Individual lives work like clockwork, and then they come together in families, communities, etc. to form a larger clockwork system. When you understand this, you can see it as a gift to you and others who have decided to reprogram their lives. With this knowledge, you know that you can change your life for the better, no matter what's going on. Here are just a few of the incredible benefits you'll notice as you start to reprogram your life by practicing the techniques we've discussed in this book.

## Gain Access to a Lifestyle Where Everything Comes Together

First of all, consider the lifestyle you'll have once you've reprogrammed your time clock. When you're feeling stressed, you'll do something healthy and productive to relax. When you're butting heads with someone, you won't waste energy trying to change them or convince them that you're right. Instead, you'll look for better solutions.
As you put all the pieces together, you'll find that you're leading a much healthier and more productive lifestyle, and you'll see more and more things fall into place for you. Your health and fitness will improve. You'll have more time for family and loved ones. Your boss will notice that you're taking more leadership initiative. You'll develop better skills at work and in your relationships.

And the best part? All of it will *feel* like everything in your life is just falling into place for you. Living this kind of lifestyle, where you focus on the present and changing yourself for the better, will actually work toward making everything come together for you.

## The World Loses Its Sting

Before, when you heard bad news at work, when someone on the street insulted you, or when you got in a fight with your spouse, it always hurt. Worse yet, it often felt like the whole world was out to get you and that it was succeeding. As you nurture and cultivate your newly reprogrammed time clock, you'll notice that it stops feeling so much like the world is against you. Things that once hurt you immensely will start to lose their sting as the world figures out that you're a different person with a healthier approach to life now.

A funny thing happens here – the world doesn't actually change for you, and the whole world won't suddenly "realize" that they can't hurt you anymore. What's changed here is you. You've changed so much that the problems, slights, and insults that once caused you so much pain are simply part of the playing field to you now. You know how you can change yourself to live better, and you know that you don't need to focus on your past mistakes or on how frustrating other people are, and that gives you a major advantage.

## Experience Less Pain and Fewer Unpleasant Surprises

As your experience of the world begins to sting less and less, you'll find that you have less emotional pain in your life and fewer unpleasant surprises as well. That's not to say that you won't have challenges in your life. In fact, you'll continue to face challenges at home, at work, and everywhere else. However, *how you see* those challenges will change dramatically.

You'll be more aware of the world around you and what's going on in the present moment, so hurdles and challenges won't surprise you nearly as much. You'll see many of them coming, and even when you do get surprised, it won't be nearly as dramatic or traumatic as it once was.

Why not? Because, when you have a surprise come your way, you won't feel blindsided. Instead, you'll see opportunities for improvement and problem solving, both of which you'll be an expert at, thanks to all of the practice you've put in as you've been reprogramming your personal time clock.

## Notice New and Wonderful Things You Never Saw Before

As this happens, you'll notice a lot of wonderful things that you never saw before. When you practice seeing the good in others, you'll find that you see more good in people and situations throughout your life. When you stop focusing on how annoyed you are that someone else won't see things your way or change for you, you'll find more appreciation for their perspective and how to work with them for the greater good. When you let go of the past, you'll see how bright the future can be.
Consider how you once walked around thinking about your past and how much you messed up. At that time, you would have never seen being laid off from work as an opportunity to use your professional connections to start your own business. You likely would've applied for unemployment benefits and started looking for a semi-decent job that would pay your bills. But if this were to happen now, you'd look at all of the avenues available to you to put yourself in a better situation and improve your future.

Likewise, as you stop looking at what you wish you could change in others, you'll start to see their unique qualities and beauties. Someone you once thought of as pigheaded and stubborn will appear strong-minded and enthusiastic. You'll start to see how the two of you can work together instead of clashing, and they may become your greatest ally at work. Who knows? One day you may even start a business with them.

Looking from this perspective will also let you see a whole different side to people, and you may be surprised at the friends you make along the way. You might even find true love where you never would've looked before as you begin to see the inner beauty of others in an entirely new way.

## Events and Situations Change, but the Clockwork Remains the Same

Life will still be unpredictable at times, but when you understand the universal clockwork system, you'll have a better view of how things and people fit together in your life. Your job may change. You may get married or have kids. You might even move to a different country.

All of these things can change, but the universal clockwork system does not. If you can keep this in perspective and continue to work on yourself, focusing on improving your life by following your newly programmed time clock, you'll continue to reap the benefits of this system throughout your life.

Now that you have a better understanding of the universal clockwork system, its benefits, and how it can lead you to a simpler, happier life, let's move on to the final chapter of this book, in which we'll go through seven specific steps to improve the clockwork events of your life. With the previous chapters about reprogramming your time clock and these steps, you should have all of the tools you need to see everything come together for you and to enjoy a better life.

***Take a few moments now to use this page as a time for self-reflection:***

_____
_____
_____
_____
_____
_____
_____
_____
_____
_____
_____
_____
_____
_____
_____
_____
_____
_____

## Chapter 9

## Seven Steps to Improve the Clockwork Events of Your Life

*"Don't carry your mistakes around with you.
Instead, place them under your feet
and use them as stepping stones."*
-Author Unknown

Are you ready to start the process of reprogramming the clockwork of your life in earnest? With the tools and exercises we've given you so far, you're already on your way. However, every journey needs a roadmap, which is what we'll create in this final chapter.

With these seven steps, you'll put what you've learned in this book into practice, and you'll improve the clockwork of the events in your life dramatically.

# 1. Reprogram Your Mind: Garbage In, Garbage Out

First, you have to reprogram the way you think. It's all too easy to focus on the garbage that you hear, see, and remember each day. However, when you can learn to let go of the past and forgive yourself, you'll stop lingering and ruminating on these things. It helps to think of negative thoughts and comments as garbage. If someone hands you a bag of garbage, what do you do? You don't hang onto it and go through it all day – you throw it away immediately.

When someone insults you, throw that thought away. When you find yourself lingering on past memories, snap yourself back into the present. Remember, the thoughts you linger on will seep into your heart, and they will affect how you see yourself and the world. So, keep the good and throw out the bad, using the techniques we went over earlier in this book.

Think of some ways as to how you can throw out the "trash":

_____
_____
_____
_____
_____
_____
_____

List some things that you see, hear or say that are trash:

_____
_____
_____
_____
_____
_____
_____
_____

## 2. Reprogram Your Heart

Next, it's time to reprogram your heart. Since you've already learned to stop lingering on negative thoughts, this will actually be a lot easier than you might think. Basically, the point of reprogramming your heart is to rid yourself of hatred, animosity, ill will toward others, deception, denial, and other negative attitudes. When you do this, you'll find that every day seems brighter and that you have an easier time waking up in the morning and getting through your day.

We went over a few tips for this earlier, including looking for the good in others, but it may also help to consider that your thoughts become actions. And, when your thoughts linger long enough, they will taint your heart. The more negativity you allow to live in your mind and heart, the more negative you will become. As a result, you'll feel more and more like you have the largest problems in the world – as if the world really is out to get you.

When you reprogram your heart, you'll feel more positive and you'll see your problems as challenges and achievable goals. Instead of focusing on what's wrong, you'll see more avenues open up to show you the way to success.

**What are some action steps you will take starting today to reprogram your heart?**

_____
_____
_____
_____
_____
_____
_____

## 3. Reprogram Your Voice

An ancient proverb says, "Out of the abundance of the heart, the mouth speaks." As you reprogram your mind and heart, you'll find yourself thinking and feeling more positive things. Let that positivity flow from your mouth. Use the exercises we talked about in the chapter about learning to control your thoughts and words here. Focus on sowing seeds of love, hope, and encouragement with others, and they'll pay you back with gratitude and positivity. As a result, you'll feel even better about yourself and your life.

The more you allow your voice to be a beacon of positivity, the less you'll linger on negativity in your life. You'll find that insults and slights slide off your back, and you'll have an easier time understanding that these negative words often come from a place of personal frustration, sadness, or anger. As you see this, you'll find it easier and easier to speak to others with kindness and to help them come to a good solution, instead of slinging insults back at them and creating a cycle of negativity.

What are 3 positive sayings you can say about others in your life?

_____
_____
_____
_____
_____
_____

## 4. Develop Techniques to Protect Your Mind, Heart, and Voice

As you've hopefully gathered thus far, this is not a quick, one-time task. Reprogramming your life takes time, and it takes consistency. Others in your life are operating under the same old norms that you were until recently, and those norms, thought patterns, and cycles tend to protect themselves with negativity and self-centered attitudes. If you can accept this and understand it, you'll be on your way, but you need to do more than just understand it.

Prepare to protect your mind, heart, and voice against negativity and backsliding every day. Some of the exercises we've discussed in this book will help you here, like replacing bad habits with good ones, noticing good qualities in others, and practicing positive activities. If you are prepared to protect your progress every day, you'll be in good shape to continue improving the clockwork events of your life.

What are 3 techniques you will use to protect your mind, heart and voice?

_____
_____
_____
_____
_____

## 5. Reprogram Your Outlook and Expectations

Remember, you can't always expect everything of everyone else. Furthermore, it's not always someone else's fault if you have a problem. If you can learn to see things from others' perspectives, you'll have changed your outlook for the better. As you understand their point of view more, it'll be easier to adjust your expectations to fit what they can actually provide.

Furthermore, you can work on reprogramming your expectations of yourself as well. In the past, you may have always dealt with bad news by getting drunk, and so that's what you've come to expect from yourself. With your newly reprogrammed time clock, you can now expect better coping mechanisms and more positive behavior in general.

In short, when you start to feel frustrated or angry at someone else, take a step back and look at the situation from a different perspective. Are you expecting things you haven't asked for and/or that the other person cannot provide? Are you expecting them to live up to the same high standards you've set for yourself? Once you see these things, you'll have an easier time finding a better solution that works for everyone instead of simply feeling frustrated that things aren't working out for you.

Do you have some unrealistic expectations of others or yourself? If so, what are they and what is a better solution for handling them?

_____
_____
_____
_____

## 6. Create a System of Self-Accountability

Want to find real success with reprogramming the clockwork events of your life? Keep yourself accountable. You can keep a daily journal in which you put your thoughts in order about what happened during the day, how you handled different situations, and how you can continue to improve.

You could also create a chart of your new habits and reactions where you check off times that you lost your temper, reacted badly, replaced a bad habit with a good one, let go of a bad memory, etc. You could even start a "Mistake Jar." Every time you make a mistake, you throw a quarter (or a dollar) in the jar, and you let it go. Then, after a certain amount of time or when the jar is full, you use that money to fund something positive in your life.

This will help you stay accountable, and it'll show you that even when you make mistakes, you'll learn from them and continue improving. Plus, if you fill up the jar, you'll get to spend that money on something like new running shoes, a session with a personal trainer, a book you've been meaning to read, or something else that will help you continue down the road to a new time clock.

## What are some ways I can hold myself accountable?

_____
_____
_____
_____
_____
_____
_____

## 7. Share Your Story with Others

Finally, don't keep it all to yourself. When you share your story with others, you'll be sharing the secret to a better life. The more people get behind reprogramming their time clocks and understanding this ancient wisdom, the better the world will be. You'll love how it feels when you reprogram your time clock to focus on the present, accept what you can't change, and improve your life, and you'll be amazed what happens when others in your life do the same thing.

As more and more people reprogram their time clocks, the universal clockwork system will continue to work as it does, but more people will be perpetuating positive cycles instead of negative ones. By sharing your story with your friends, family, and others, you'll be enacting a positive change in your world.

What are a few ways I can share my story and this book with others I love?

_____
_____
_____
_____
_____
_____
_____
_____

# *Conclusion*

Now that you've read this book, you know just how simple it can be to change your life for the better. You know that you don't need to start all over and do it all right the first time, and you know that you don't need to erase past mistakes or change your whole situation to have a positive experience every day.

When you realize that focusing on the past doesn't help you but actually hurts you, and you learn to let go of it, you can experience real, significant change in very little time. And, if you use this book as a guide and refer back to it whenever you're having trouble, you'll have a handy tool at your fingertips to help you stay the course.

## Be Patient and Stay the Course

Before we leave you, we do want to stress once more that this is not a one-and-done fix. Reprogramming your time clock is not like setting an alarm clock when you have to get up for work. Instead, it's a lot like adjusting to getting up early in the morning when you're used to staying up late at night and sleeping in. Getting up early allows you to be more productive, to do more with your day, and to have more time for your friends and family, but it takes some time to adjust to a different schedule, right?

Furthermore, if you don't continue to practice getting up early in the morning, as well as getting to bed on time at night, it'll continue to be difficult, and you'll eventually go back to your old ways of wasting the day in bed. However, if you work on your sleep schedule consistently, you'll enjoy a lot more quality time with the people you love every day.

Reprogramming your personal time clock to work with the universal clockwork system works much like this. If you practice the things you need to do to maintain a new perspective, to keep your mind, heart, and voice positive, and to keep your new programming in good working order, you'll reap incredible benefits.

If you do slip up, though, don't beat yourself up. You're human, and the traits that we discussed earlier in this book are very human ones. It's natural to blame someone else to protect yourself. It's natural to wince and ruminate when you remember mistakes you've made. And it's natural to feel frustrated and angry when others don't do things that you think are perfectly logical and reasonable.

If you're patient with yourself and you give yourself time to change, you'll notice massive improvements. Better yet, you'll notice those improvements before you know it. With a little bit of patience and forgiveness for yourself, you can enjoy all of the benefits of the universal clockwork system in your life.

And, with this book, you have a reference that you can come back to time and again whenever you need help or reminders. You can even keep it with you as a reminder that you're doing a great job and that you need to keep practicing your new programming to succeed throughout your life. To further the impact of this book on your life, I recommend using the Reprogramming in Process Journal. I fully believe in you and I believe that you have the strength and power to make your life one to remember!

Remember, YOU GOT THIS!!!

*"I can choose to let it define me,
confine me, refine me, or outshine me,
or I can choose to move on
and leave it behind me."*
-Author Unknown

## Works Cited

You Can't Change Others: Letting People Be
https://psychcentral.com/blog/archives/2013/05/14/you-cant-change-others-letting-people-be/

How to Let Go and Forgive
https://zenhabits.net/how-to-let-go-and-forgive/

How to Let Go of Past Hurts
http://m.wikihow.com/Let-Go-of-Past-Hurts

40 Ways to Let Go and Feel Less Pain
http://tinybuddha.com/blog/40-ways-to-let-go-and-feel-less-pain/

What Not To Do If You've Been Cheated On: Pointers for Chumps
http://www.huffingtonpost.com/tracy-schorn/cheated-on-tips_b_1987271.html

Why Ruminating is Unhealthy and How to Stop
https://psychcentral.com/blog/archives/2011/01/20/why-ruminating-is-unhealthy-and-how-to-stop/

How To Stop Focusing On The Past
http://www.joyfulmeanings.com/blog/2012/01/21/how-to-stop-focusing-on-the-past/

10 Things You Must Accept And 10 Things You Must Change In Your Life
http://elitedaily.com/life/10-things-you-must-accept-and-10-things-you-must-change-in-your-life/609001/

How To Accept What You Can't Change
http://thoughtcatalog.com/briannaewiest/2013/05/how-to-accept-what-you-cant-change/

How To Tell If You Have A Food Addiction-And 8 Ways To Regain Control


How to Conquer Your Compulsions
http://www.womansday.com/health-fitness/womens-health/how-to/a5583/how-to-conquer-your-compulsions-116339/

12 Ways to Beat Addiction
https://psychcentral.com/blog/archives/2010/06/05/12-ways-to-beat-addiction/